English - Marathi

#1

lion
लायन्
सिंह

#2

sheep
शीप्
मेंढां

#3

frog
फ्रॉग्
बेडूक

#4

jackal
जॅकल
कोल्हा

#5

owl
आऊल्
घुबड

#6

penguin
पेंग्वेन
पेंग्वेन

#7

mole
मोल्
घुंडा

#8

insect
इन्सेक्ट्
किडा

#9

elephant
एलेफन्ट्
हत्ती

#10

turkey
टर्-की
टकी

#11

firefly
फायर-फ्लाय
फायरफ्लाय

#12

ostrich
ऑस्ट्रेच्
शहामृग

#13

peacock
पीकॉक्
मोर

#14

parrot
पॅरट्
पोपट

#15

woodpecker
वुड-पेकर
लाकूडपेकर

#16

pigeon
पिजन्
कबूतर

hawk
हॉक्
बहिरी ससाणा

jaguar
जॅग्वार
जग्वार

deer
डिअर्
हारण

cockroach
कॉक-रोच
झुरळ

otter
ऑटर
ऊद

snake
स्नेक्
साप

cow
काउ
गाय

boar
बोअर्
डुक्कर

camel
कॅमल्
उंट

vulture
वल्चर्
गिधाड

dingo
डिंगा
डिंगा

pig
पिग्
डुक्कर

eagle
इगल्
गरुड

mare
मॅर्
घोडी

quail
केल्
लावा

porcupine
पॉरक्युपाइन्
साळेंदर

hamster
हॅमस्टर
हॅमस्टर

crow
क्रो
कावळा

llama
लामा
लामा

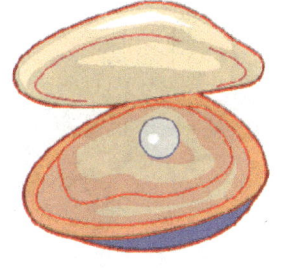

oyster
ऑयस्टर्
शिंपला

worm
वॉर्म्
जंत

kitten
किटन्
मांजरीचे पिल्लू

flamingo
फ्लॉमिनगो
फ्लोमेंगो

bison
बायसन
बायसन

zebra
झेब्रा
झेब्रा

rabbit
रॅबेट्
ससा

sparrow
स्पॅरो
चिमणी

mouse
माउस
उंदार

panda
पॅण्डा
पांडा

starfish
स्टार-फिश
स्टारफेश

bird
बड्
पक्षी

squid
स्क्वेड
स्क्वेड

#49	#50	#51	#52

lizard लिझड् सरड	puppy पप्पी लहान कुत्रा	ant ॲन्ट् मुंगी	stork स्टॉर्क सारस

#53	#54	#55	#56

animal ॲनेमल् प्राणी	octopus ऑक्-टो-पस ऑक्टोपस	wolf वुल्फ लांडगा	mermaid ममेड् मत्स्यकन्या

#57	#58	#59	#60

seagull सी-गल समुद्रपक्षी	whale व्हेल् तोमंगल	fish फिश् मासा	squirrel स्क्वेरल् खार

#61	#62	#63	#64

pelican पोलेकन् पोलेकन	turtle टर्टल् कासव	rat रॅट् उंदीर	gecko गका गका

#65  **butterfly** बटरफ्लाय् फुलपाखरू	#66  **grasshopper** ग्रॅस-हॉपर मांत्रेक	#67  **goose** गूस हंस	#68  **mice** माइस् उदार
#69  **cat** कॅट् मांजर	#70  **rooster** रू-स्टर् कोंबडा	#71  **bee** बी मधमाशी	#72  **raven** रेव्हन कावळा
#73  **dolphin** डॉल्फिन् डॉल्फिन	#74  **reindeer** रेनडेअर् रेनडेअर	#75  **emu** इमू इमू	#76  **horse** हॉस् घोडा
#77  **chicken** चिकन् कोंबडी	#78  **giraffe** जिरॅफ जिराफ	#79  **dog** डॉग् कुत्रा	#80  **walrus** वॉलूस समुद्री गायी

#81

hedgehog
हेड्-ज-हॉग्
साळींदर

#82

wasp
वॉस्प
गांधळ

#83

dove
डव
पारवा

#84

shark
शाक्
शार्क

#85

moth
मॉथ
पतंग

#86

duck
डक्
बदक

#87

dinosaur
डाय-नो-सॉर
डायनासोर

#88

falcon
फालकन
फाल्कन

#89

koala
कोआला
कोआला

#90

fox
फॉक्स्
कोल्हा

#91

dragonfly
ड्रॅ-गन-फ्लाय
ड्रॅगनफ्लाय

#92

crab
क्रॅब्
खेकडा

#93

alligator
ऑलि-गेटर्
मगर

#94

hippopotamus
हिप्पो-पॉ-टॅमस्
जलहस्ती

#95

toad
टोअड्
भोवरा

#96

gorilla
गोरिल्ला
गोरिल्ला

#97
chameleon
कॅमेलेयन
गिरागेट

#98
clam
क्लॅम्
शिंपली

#99
ladybug
लेडी-बग
भुंगा

#100
tiger
टायगर
वाघ

#101
antelope
ऑंटे-लो-ऍप
काळवीट

#102
moose
मूस
मूस

#103
kangaroo
कॅन्-ग-रू
कांगारू

#104
ox
आँक्स
बैल

#105
dragon
ड्रॅगन
ड्रॅगन

#106
lobster
लॉब-स्टर
लॉबस्टर

#107
spider
स्पायडर्
कोळी

#108
yak
यॅक
याक

#109
mongoose
मॅंगूस
मुंगूस

#110
iguana
इगुआना
इगुआना

#111
centipede
सेंटी-पिड्
शतपदी

#112
unicorn
यु-नि-कॉन्
युनेकॉर्न

#113

swan
स्वॉन्
हंस

#114

nightingale
नाइटिन्गेल
नाइटिंगेल

#115

goat
गोट्
शेळी

#116

monkey
मन्की
माकड

#117

snail
स्नेल्
गोगलगाय

#118

jellyfish
जेली-फिश
जोलोफेश

#119

raccoon
रॅकून
रॅकून

#120

orca
ऑका
ओका

#121

monster
मॉन्स्टर्
राक्षस

#122

beetle
बीटल
गांडूळ

#123

mosquito
मॉस्किटो
डास

#124

caterpillar
कॅटर-पिलर
अळी

#125

cheetah
चीता
चित्ता

#126

hen
हन्
कोंबडी

#127

candy
कॅन्डी
गोळी

#128

yolk
यो-ल्क
जदा

#129  **watermelon** वॉ-टर्-मेलन् कालेंगड	#130  **nectar** नेक्टर अमृत	#131 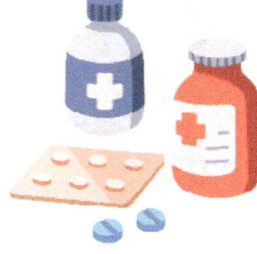 **medicine** मोडीसेन् औषध	#132  **waffle** वाफल वायफळ बडबड
#133  **pineapple** पायनॅपल् अननस	#134  **shrimp** श्रिम्प कोळंबी	#135  **gourd** गॉड लोकी	#136  **raspberry** रॅस्बेरी रास्पबेरी
#137  **blueberry** ब्ल्यूबेरी ब्लूबेरी	#138  **grape** ग्रेप् द्राक्ष	#139  **avocado** ऑव्होकॅडो अवोकाडो	#140  **almond** ऑल्मंड बदाम
#141  **grapes** ग्रेप्स द्राक्ष	#142  **sandwich** सॅन्डावेच सॅंडावेच	#143  **plum** प्लम् आलुबुखार	#144  **jelly** जेली जेली

peanut
पीनट्
शेंगदाणा

carrot
कॅरट्
गाजर

egg
एग्
अंडं

pancake
पॅन-केक
पॅनकेक

tangerine
टॅन्जारेन्
संत्र

noodles
नूडल्स्
नूडल्स

fruit
फ्रूट
फळ

yogurt
यो-गट्
दही

nut
नट
नट

honey
हनी
मध

peach
पीच्
पीच

spinach
स्पि-नॅच
पालक

zucchini
झुकीनी
भोपळा

pear
पिअर्
नाशपती

donut
डोनट
डोनट

beer
बीअर
बिअर

cucumber
क्यूकम्बर्
काकडी

apple
ॲपल्
सफरचंद

meal
मिल
जेवण

lemon
लेमन्
लिंबू

pizza
पिइझा
पिइझा

butter
बटर
लोणी

cake
केक्
केक

grapefruit
ग्रेप-फ्रूट
द्राक्षफळ

wheat
व्हीट्
गहू

bean
बीन्
शेंग

water
वॉटर्
पाणी

soup
सूप्
सूप

salt
सॉल्ट
मीठ

cauliflower
कॉ-लि-फ्लॉवर्
फुलकोबी

doughnut
डोनट
डोनट

seafood
सी-फूड
सीफूड

#177

tomato
टोमॅटो
टोमॅटो

#178

garlic
गालिक
लसूण

#179

jam
जॅम्
जाम

#180

salad
सॅलड
कोशंबीर

#181

popsicles
पॉप्सिकल्स्
पॉपासेकल्स

#182

coconut
कोकोनट्
नारळ

#183

melon
मेलन
खरबूज

#184

artichoke
आर्टिचोक
आर्टिचोक

#185

tea
टी
चहा

#186

celery
सेलरी
अजमोदा

#187

meat
माट्
मांस

#188

yam
यॅम
याम

#189

dinner
डिनर
रात्रीचं जेवण

#190

eggplant
एग्प्लॅन्ट्
वांगी

#191

jellybean
जेली-बी-न
जेलीबीन

#192

onion
आनेयन्
कांदा

#193

banana
बॅनाना
केळ

#194

walnut
वॉल-नट
अक्रोड

#195

cupcake
कप-केक
कपकक

#196

rice
राइस
तांदूळ

#197

milk
मिल्क्
दूध

#198

turnip
टानेप्
मुळा

#199

sunflower
सनफ्लॉवर्
सूयेमुखी

#200

sausage
सॉसेज्
सॉसेज

#201

olive
ऑलेव
ऑलेव्ह

#202

coffee
कॉफी
कॉफी

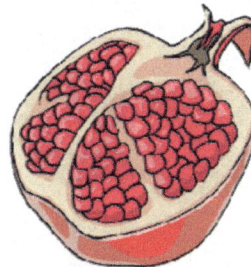

#203

pomegranate
पॉमग्रॅनेट्
डाळ्ळेंब

#204

broccoli
ब्रॉकली
ब्रोकाली

#205

chocolate
चॉकलेट्
चॉकलेट

#206

tuna
टूना
ट्यूना

#207

breakfast
ब्रेक-फास्ट
नाश्ता

#208

nutmeg
नट-मेग
जायफळ

#209

pumpkin
पम्प-किन
भोपळा

#210

peas
पिज्
मटार

#211

icecream
आईस-क्रिम्
आइसक्रीम

#212

vegetable
वेजिटेबल्
भाजी

#213

bread
ब्रेड्
ब्रेड

#214

pie
पाय्
पाई

#215

radish
रॉडेश
मूळा

#216

strawberry
स्ट्रॉ-बेरी
स्ट्रॉबेरी

#217

cabbage
कॅबेज
कोबी

#218

asparagus
अ-स्पे-रॅ-गस
शतावरी

#219

apricot
ए-प्रि-कॉट
जदोळू

#220

food
फूड
अन्न

#221

juice
ज्यूस्
रस

#222

sugar
शुगर
साखर

#223

cheese
चाज्
चीज

#224

acorn
एकॉन
एकोने

#225

lemonade
लेम-नेड
लिंबूपाणी

#226

lettuce
लेट-ट्यूस
सलाड

#227

wine
वाइन
द्राक्षारस

#228

lime
लाइम
लिंबू

#229

kale
केल
काळे

#230

mushroom
मश्रूम्
मशरूम

#231

parsnip
पास्त्रेप
पासीनेप

#232

corn
कॉन्
मका

#233

ham
हॅम्
हॅम

#234

cookie
कुकी
कुकी

#235

lychee
ली-ची
लीची

#236

kiwi
की-वी
किवी

#237

potato
पोटॅटो
बटाटा

#238

pepper
पे-प्पर
मिरा

#239

noodle
नूडल
नूडल

#240

mango
मॅन्गो
आंबा

#241	#242	#243	#244
zero झी-रो शून्य	one वन् एक	two टू दोन	three थ्री तीन

#245	#246	#247	#248
four फोअर चार	five फाइव्ह पाच	six सिक्स् सहा	seven सेव्हन सात

#249	#250	#251	#252
eight एट् आठ	nine नाइन् नऊ	ten टेन् दहा	eleven इले-वन अकरा

#253	#254	#255	#256
twelve ट्वेल्व बारा	thirteen थर्टीन तेरा	fourteen फो-र्टीन चौदा	fifteen फिफ्टीन पंधरा

#257
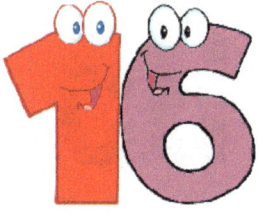
sixteen
सिक्स्टीन
साळा

#258
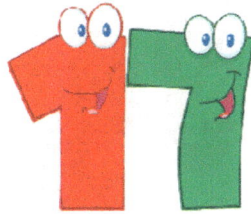
seventeen
सेवन-टीन
सतरा

#259

eighteen
एइ-टीन
अठरा

#260

nineteen
नाइन-टीन
एकोणीस

#261
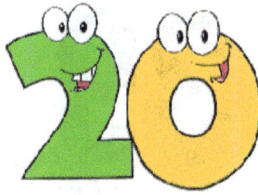
twenty
ट्वेन्-टी
वीस

#262

twenty one
ट्वेन्-टी-वन्
एकवीस

#263

twenty two
ट्वेन्-टी-टू
बावीस

#264

twenty three
ट्वेन्-टी-श्री
तेवीस

#265

twenty four
ट्वेन्-टी-फोअर
चोवीस

#266

twenty five
ट्वेन्-टी-फाइव्ह
पंचवीस

#267

twenty six
ट्वेन्-टी-सिक्स्
सहावीस

#268

twenty seven
ट्वेन्-टी-सेव्ह्न
सत्तावीस

#269

twenty eight
ट्वेन्-टी-एट्
अठ्ठावीस

#270

twenty nine
ट्वेन्-टी-नाइन्
एकोणतीस

#271

thirty
थटी
तीस

#272

thirty one
थटी-वन्
एकतीस

#273

32
thirty two
थर्टी-टू
बत्तीस

#274

33
thirty three
थर्टी-थ्री
तेहतीस

#275

34
thirty four
थर्टी-फोअर
चोतीस

#276

35
thirty five
थर्टी-फाइव्ह
पस्तीस

#277

36
thirty six
थर्टी-सिक्स्
छत्तीस

#278

37
thirty seven
थर्टी-सेव्हन्
सदोतीस

#279

38
thirty eight
थर्टी-एट्
अडतीस

#280

39
thirty nine
थर्टी-नाइन्
एकोणचाळीस

#281

40
forty
फॉर्टी
चाळीस

#282

41
forty one
फॉर्टी-वन्
एकचाळीस

#283

42
forty two
फॉर्टी-टू
बेचाळीस

#284

43
forty three
फॉर्टी-थ्री
त्रेचाळीस

#285

44
forty four
फॉर्टी-फोअर
चव्वेचाळीस

#286

45
forty five
फॉर्टी-फाइव्ह
पंचचाळीस

#287

46
forty six
फॉर्टी-सिक्स्
शेहचाळीस

#288

47
forty seven
फॉर्टी-सेव्हन्
सत्तेचाळीस

#289 **48** forty eight फॉर्टी-एट् अठ्ठेचाळीस	#290 **49** forty nine फॉर्टी-नाइन् एकोणपन्नास	#291 **50** fifty फिफ्टी पन्नास	#292 **51** fifty one फिफ्टी-वन् एक्कावन्न
#293 **52** fifty two फिफ्टी-टू बावन्न	#294 **53** fifty three फिफ्टी-थ्री त्रेपन्न	#295 **54** fifty four फिफ्टी-फोअर चोपन्न	#296 **55** fifty five फिफ्टी-फाइव्ह पंचावन्न
#297 **56** fifty six फिफ्टी-सिक्स् छप्पन्न	#298 **57** fifty seven फिफ्टी-सेव्हन् सत्तावन्न	#299 **58** fifty eight फिफ्टी-एट् अठ्ठावन्न	#300 **59** fifty nine फिफ्टी-नाइन् एकोणसाठ
#301 **60** sixty सिक्स्टी साठ	#302 **61** sixty one सिक्स्टी-वन् एकसाठ	#303 **62** sixty two सिक्स्टी-टू बावसाठ	#304 **63** sixty three सिक्स्टी-थ्री त्रेसष्ठ

64 #305 sixty four सिक्स्टी-फोअर चौसष्ट	**65** #306 sixty five सिक्स्टी-फाइव्ह पासष्ट	**66** #307 sixty six सिक्स्टी-सिक्स् सहासष्ट	**67** #308 sixty seven सिक्स्टी-सेव्हन सत्तासष्ट
68 #309 sixty eight सिक्स्टी-एट् अडूसष्ट	**69** #310 sixty nine सिक्स्टी-नाइन् एकोणसत्तर	**70** #311 seventy सेव्हन्टी सत्तर	**71** #312 seventy one सेव्हन्टी-वन् एकाहत्तर
72 #313 seventy two सेव्हन्टी-टू बहात्तर	**73** #314 seventy three सेव्हन्टी-श्री त्र्याहत्तर	**74** #315 seventy four सेव्हन्टी-फोअर चोपन्न	**75** #316 seventy five सेव्हन्टी-फाइव्ह पंच्याहत्तर
76 #317 seventy six सेव्हन्टी-सिक्स् शहात्तर	**77** #318 seventy seven सेव्हन्टी-सेव्हन सत्याहत्तर	**78** #319 seventy eight सेव्हन्टी-एट् अठ्ठ्याहत्तर	**79** #320 seventy nine सेवेन-टी नाइन एकोणऐंशी

#321 **80** eighty एइटी ऐंशी	#322 **81** eighty one एइटी वन एक्याऐंशी	#323 **82** eighty two एइटी टू ब्याऐंशी	#324 **83** eighty three एइटी श्री त्र्याऐंशी
#325 **84** eighty four एइटी फोर चौर्याऐंशी	#326 **85** eighty five एइटी फाइव्ह पंच्याऐंशी	#327 **86** eighty six एइटी सिक्स शहाऐंशी	#328 **87** eighty seven एइटी-सेव्हन सत्याऐंशी
#329 **88** eighty eight एइटी एट अठ्याऐंशी	#330 **89** eighty nine एइटी नाइन एकोणनव्वद	#331 **90** ninety नाइंटी नव्वद	#332 **91** ninety one नाइंटी वन एक्क्याण्णव
#333 **92** ninety two नाइंटी टू ब्याण्णव	#334 **93** ninety three नाइंटी श्री त्र्याण्णव	#335 **94** ninety four नाइंटी फोर चौर्याण्णव	#336 **95** ninety five नाइंटी फाइव्ह पंच्याण्णव

#337

96

ninety six
नाइंटी सिक्स
शहाण्णव

#338

97

ninety seven
नाइंटी सेव्हन
सत्त्याण्णव

#339

98

ninety eight
नाइंटी एइट
अठ्ठ्याण्णव

#340

99

ninety nine
नाइंटी नाइन
एकोणशे

#341

100

hundred
हंड्रेड
शंभर

#342

1000

thousand
थाउजंड
हजार

#343

shoulder
शोल्डर्
खांदा

#344

heart
हाट्
हृदय

#345

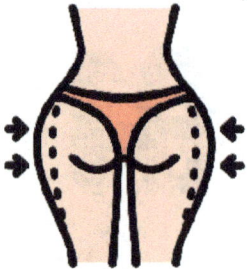

hips
हिप्स
कूल्हे

#346

eye
आय
डोळा

#347

face
फस्
चहरा

#348

toes
टाएस
पायाची बोटं

#349

hip
हिप्
नितंब

#350

wig
विग्
विग

#351

thumb
थम्ब्
अंगठा

#352

nose
नोझ्
नाक

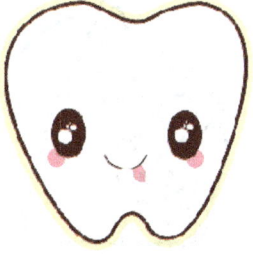 #353	 #354	 #355	 #356
teeth टीथ् दात	tooth टूथ् दात	shoulders शोल्डस खांद	elbow एल्बो कोपर
 #357	 #358	 #359	 #360
leg लग् पाय	knees नीज गुडघे	tongue टन्ग् जीभ	muscle मसल् स्नायू
 #361	 #362	 #363	 #364
fin फिन् पंख	neck नेक् मान	forehead फॉरहेड कपाळ	hands हॅन्ड्स हात
 #365	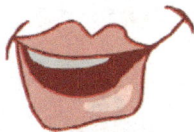 #366	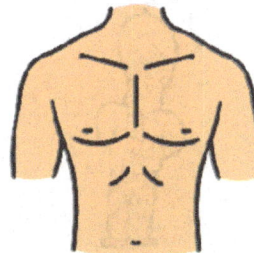 #367	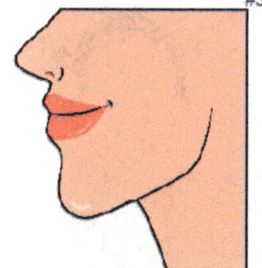 #368
legs लग्ज पाय	lips लिप्स ओठ	chest चस्ट छाती	chin चिन् हनुवटी

head
हेड्
डोकें

bone
बोन्
हाड

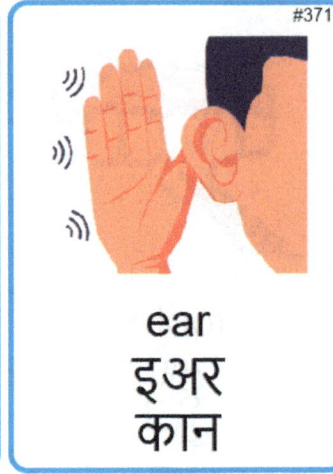

ear
इअर
कान

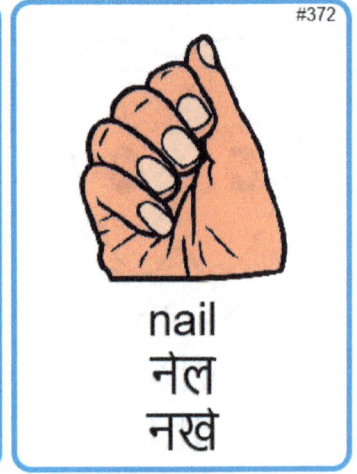

nail
नेल
नख

throat
थ्रोट
घसा

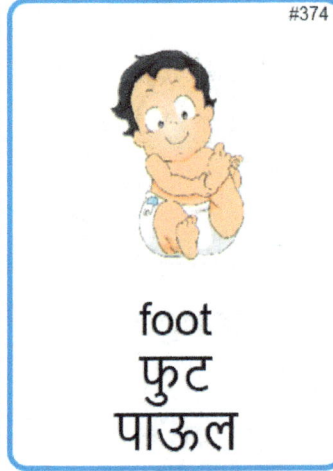

foot
फुट
पाऊल

wing
विंग
पंख

tail
टेल्
शेपूट

beard
बेअर्ड्
दाढी

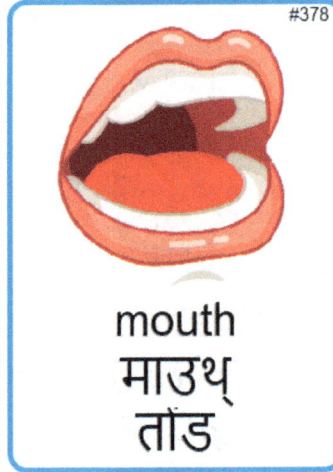

mouth
माउथ्
तोंड

stomach
स्टमक
पोट

brain
ब्रेन्
मेंदू

feet
फीट
पाय

waist
वेस्ट
कंबर

hair
हेअर्
केस

cheeks
चीक्स
गाल

body
बॉ-डी
शरीर

blood
ब्लड्
रक्त

eyebrows
आय-ब्रोज
भुवया

people
पीपल्
लोक

girl
गर्ल्
मुलगी

niece
नीस
पुतणी

children
चिल्ड्रन्
मुलं

grandson
ग्रॅड-सन
नातू

boyfriend
बॉयफ्रेंड
प्रियकर

brother
ब्रदस्
भाऊ

grandmother
ग्रॅड-मदर
आजी

kid
किड
मुल

stepson
स्टेप-सन
सावत्र मुलगा

girlfriend
गर्ल-फ्रेंड
मैत्रीण

uncle
अंकल
काका

mom
मॉम्
आई

#401

friend
फ्रेंड्
मित्र

#402

man
मॅन्
माणूस

#403

nephew
नेफ्यू
पुतण्या

#404

stepmother
स्टेप-मदर
सावत्र आई

#405

granddaughter
ग्रँड-डॉटर
नात

#406

daughter
डॉ-टर
मुलगा

#407

wife
वाइफ
पत्नी

#408

lady
लेडी
स्त्री

#409

stepdaughter
स्टेप-डॉटर
सावत्र मुलगी

#410

family
फॅमेली
कुटुंब

#411

son
सन
मुलगा

#412

mother
मदर
आई

#413

cousin
काझिन
चुलत भाऊ

#414

kids
किड्स्
मुलं

#415

child
चाइल्ड
मूल

#416

boy
बॉय्
मुलगा

#417

sister
सिस्टर्
बहीण

#418

member
मेम-बर
सदस्य

#419

father
फादर्
वडील

#420

toddler
टॉडलर्
लहान मूल

#421

dad
डॅड्
बाबा

#422

woman
वूमन
स्त्री

#423

group
ग्रूप्
गट

#424

aunt
आंट
आत्या

#425

toy
टॉय्
खेळणं

#426

hatchet
हॅचेट
कुंडी

#427

equipment
इक्विप-मेंट
उपकरण

#428

newspaper
न्यूज-पेपर
वृत्तपत्र

#429

chalk
चॉक
खडू

#430

mug
मग
मग

#431

seeds
सिड्स्
बियाणं

#432

candle
कॅन्डल्
मेणबत्ती

towel
टॉ-वेल्
टॉवेल

bottle
बॉटल्
बाटली

wreath
रिथ्
पुष्पहार

javelin
जॅव्ह-लिन
भाला

duster
डस्टर
डस्टर

lantern
लॅन्टन्
कंदील

fan
फॅन
पंखा

collar
कॉलर्
कॉलर

ax
ॲक्स्
कुऱ्हाड

fireplace
फायरप्लेस्
अंगठा

umbrella
अॅम्-ब्रेला
छत्री

toilet
टॉयलेट्
टॉयलेट

cleanser
क्लेन्सर
क्लेन्सर

spatula
स्पॅचुला
पळी

bowtie
बो-टाय
बो टाय

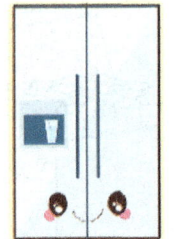

refrigerator
रेफ्रिजरेटर
फ्रिज

shirt
शट्
शटें

barrel
बै-रल
बॅरल

bed
बेड्
खाट

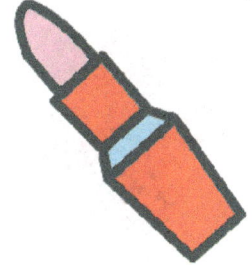

lipstick
लिपास्टेक्
लिपास्टेक

hammock
हॅमॉक
झूला

teapot
टीपॉट्
चहादाणी

boot
बूट्
बूट

paintbrush
पेंट्-ब्रश्
पेंटब्रश

key
की
चावी

bag
बॅग्
पिशवी

anvil
अॅन्वेल
एव्होल

kitchen
किचन्
स्वयंपाकघर

pin
पिन्
पिन

rope
रोप
दोरी

lamp
लॅम्प्
दिवा

carpet
कापेट्
गालिचा

#465

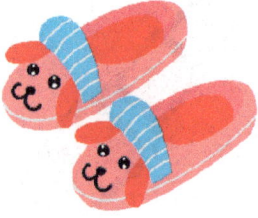

slippers
स्लिपस्
चप्पल

#466

utensil
युटे-नासेल
भांडी

#467

pan
पॅन्
पॅन

#468

yarn
यान्
सूत

#469

envelope
एनवेलोप
लिफाफा

#470

eraser
इ-रे-सर
इरेजर

#471

computer
कंप्युटर
संगणक

#472

bucket
बकट्
बादली

#473

raincoat
रेन-कोट
पावसाळी कोट

#474

cash
कॅश
रोख

#475

bouquet
बुक
पुष्पगुच्छ

#476

crayon
क्रेयॉन्
खडू

#477

tent
टेंट्
तंबू

#478

suitcase
सूटकेस्
सुटकेस

#479

ring
रिंग
अंगठी

#480

ruler
रूलर्
फूटपट्टी

#481  **kettle** केटल केटल	#482  **pot** पॉट् भांडे	#483  **dice** डायस् फासे	#484 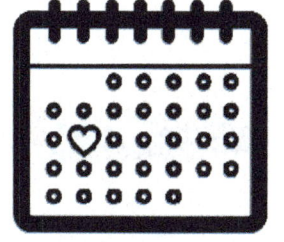 **calendar** कॅलेंडर् दिनदर्शिका
#485  **houseplant** हाउस-प्लांट घरगुती वनस्पती	#486  **basket** बास्केट टोपली	#487  **crayons** क्रेयोन्स क्रेयॉन	#488 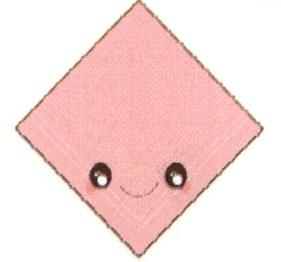 **handkerchief** हॅड्करचिफ् रुमाल
#489  **hat** हॅट् टोपी	#490  **leash** लीश पट्टा	#491  **vest** वेस्ट् बानेयान	#492  **wheelbarrow** व्हील-बॅरो एकचाकी हातगाडी
#493  **firewood** फायरवूड सरपण	#494  **socks** सॉक्स् मोजे	#495  **magazine** मॅगझीन मासिक	#496  **mirror** मिरर् आरसा

#497

fabric
फॅब्रेक
फॉब्रेक

#498
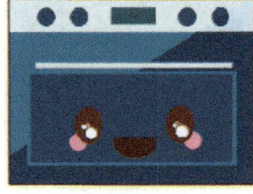
oven
ओव्हन्
ओव्हन

#499

bowl
बोल्
वाटी

#500

mat
मॅट्
चटइे

#501

tray
ट्रे
तांट

#502

scissors
सिझस्
कात्री

#503

pitcher
पिचर
घड्या

#504

blanket
ब्लॉन्-किट्
ब्लॉकेट

#505

tire
टायर्
टायरं

#506

jacket
जॅकेट्
जॅकेट

#507

shovel
शव्हल्
फावडा

#508

photo
फोटो
छायाचेत्र

#509

cup
कप
कप

#510

diamond
डायमन्ड्
हिरा

#511

compass
कम्पास्
दिशादशेक

#512

ink
इन्क्
शाई

#513  **wrench** रेंच पाना	#514 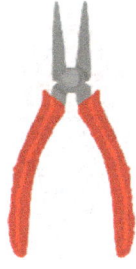 **pliers** प्लायस प्लायस
#515 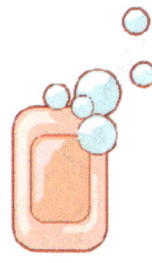 **soap** सोप साबण	#516  **book** बुक् पुस्तक
#517  **pencil** पेनसेल् पोन्सेल	#518  **earring** इयररेंग् कानातले
#519  **tool** टूल साधन	#520  **flashlight** फ्लॅशलाइट विजेरी
#521  **gasoline** गॅसोलीन् पेट्रोल	#522  **stockings** स्टॉकेंग्ज् मोज
#523  **chisel** चिसल छेन्नी	#524  **cap** कॅप टोपी
#525  **spoon** स्पून चमचा	#526  **calculator** कॅल्क्युलेटर् कॅल्क्युलेटर
#527  **shoe** शू जोडा	#528  **curtains** कर-टन्स पडद

#529

teacup
टी-कप्
चहाचा कप

#530

broom
ब्रूम्
झाडू

#531

torch
टॉर्च्
मशाल

#532

chainsaw
चेन-सॉ
चेनसां

#533
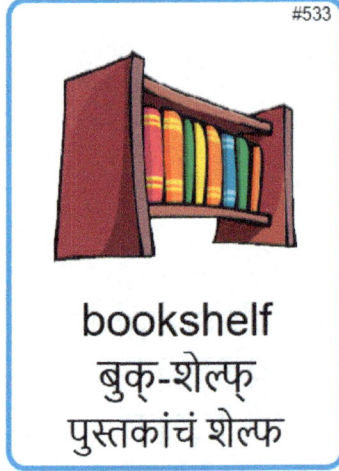
bookshelf
बुक-शेल्फ्
पुस्तकांचं शेल्फ

#534

chair
चेअर्
खुर्ची

#535

picture
पिक्चर्
चित्र

#536

hammer
हॅमर
हातोडा

#537

cage
केज्
पिंजरा

#538

napkin
नॅपोकेन
रुमाल

#539
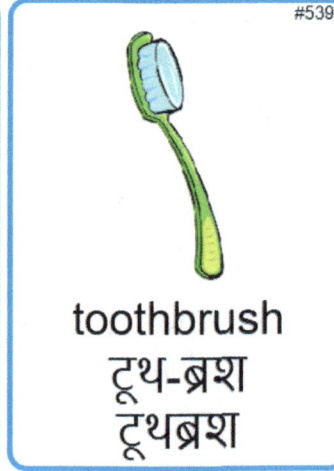
toothbrush
टूथ-ब्रश
टूथब्रश

#540

pearls
पल्स्
मोतीं

#541

backpack
बॅक-पॅक्
बॅकपॅक

#542

toaster
टोस्टर
टोस्टर

#543

cushion
कु-शन
कुशन

#544
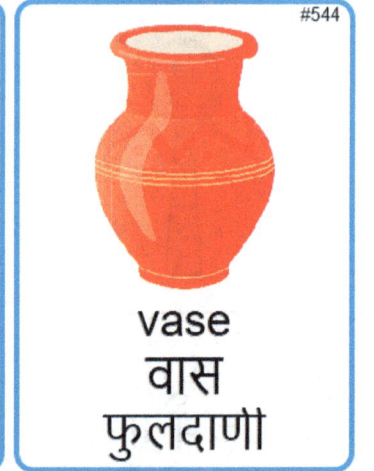
vase
वास
फुलदाणी

#545

chalkboard
चॉकबोड्
फळा

#546

shield
शिल्ड
ढाल

#547

undershirt
अंडर-शर्ट
संडो

#548

utensils
यूटेन्सिल्स्
भांडा

#549

prize
प्राइज्
बक्षीस

#550

scarf
स्काफ्
मफलर

#551

belt
बेल्ट्
पट्टा

#552

coat
काट्
काट

#553

box
बॉक्स्
पेटी

#554

glass
ग्लास्
काच

#555

hanger
हॅंगर
हंगर

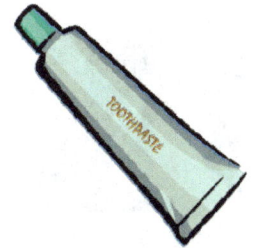

#556

toothpaste
टूथ-पेस्ट
टूथपेस्ट

#557

pants
पॅंट्स
पॅन्ट

#558

apron
एप्रन
अॅप्रन

#559

bassinet
बॉसेनेट
बासेनेट

#560

saw
सॉ
पाहिल

#561

shorts
शॉर्ट्स्
हाफपॅंट

#562

necklace
नेकलेस्
माळ

#563

clothes
क्लोथ्स
कपड

#564

fork
फॉंक
कांटा

#565

blender
ब्लेंडर
ब्लेंडर

#566

typewriter
टाइप-राय-टर
टायपरायटर

#567

gift
गिफ्ट्
भेट

#568

television
टेलिव्हिजन
दूरदर्शन

#569

closet
क्लॉजेट्
कपाट

#570

rake
रेक
खुरपणी

#571

brush
ब्रश
ब्रश

#572
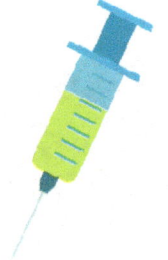
syringe
सिरिंज्
सुई

#573

letter
लेटर्
पत्र

#574

flag
फ्लॅग्
ध्वज

#575

vacuum
व्हॅक्युम
व्हॅक्यूम

#576

lid
लिड्
झाकण

#577  **saucer** सॉ-सर बशी	#578  **mitten** मिटी-न मिटन	#579  **quill** क्विल क्विल	#580 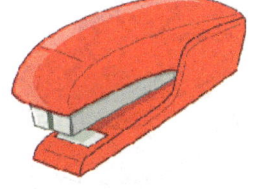 **stapler** स्टेप-लर स्टेपलर
#581  **shoes** शूज् बूट	#582  **silk** सिल्क रेशीम	#583  **radio** रेडियो रेडिओ	#584  **inkpad** इंक-पॅड इंकपॅड
#585  **keychain** की-चेन कीचेन	#586  **quilt** क्विल्ट रजाई	#587 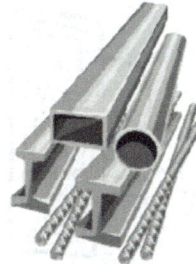 **metal** मेटल धातू	#588  **zipper** झिपर जिपर
#589  **microwave** मायक्रो-वेव मायक्रोवेव्ह	#590  **glue** ग्लू गोंद	#591  **telephone** टेलिफोन टेलिफोन	#592  **jar** जार किलाकिल

#593

bathtub
बाथटब्
बाथटब

#594

desk
डेस्क्
टेबल

#595

doll
डॉल्
बाहुली

#596

bin
बिन्
कचराकुंडी

#597

sweater
स्वेटर्
स्वेटर

#598

cupboard
कबड
कपाट

#599

dish
डिश
ताट

#600

diaper
डायपर
लंगोट

#601

vaccine
व्हॅक्सीन्
लस

#602

keyhole
की-होल
कोहोल

#603

phone
फोन
फोन

#604

easel
इजल
चित्रफलक

#605
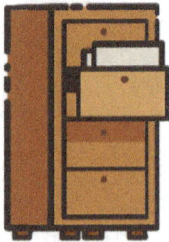
cabinet
कॅबिनेट
कॅबिनेट

#606
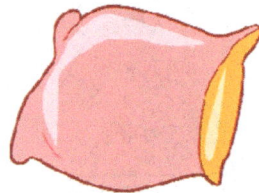
pillow
पिलो
उशी

#607

paper
पपर्
कागद

#608

notebook
नोट-बुक
वही

#609

jug
जग्
जग

#610

clock
क्लॉक्
घड्याळ

#611

trousers
ट्राउ-झर्स
पॅंट

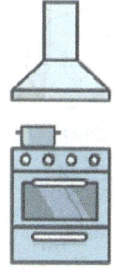

#612

stove
स्टोव्ह्
चूल

#613

broomstick
ब्रूम-स्टिक
झाडू

#614

table
टेबल
टेबल

#615

screwdriver
स्क्रू-ड्राय-वर
स्क्रू ड्रायव्हर

#616

slipper
स्लिपर
चप्पल

#617

money
मनी
पैसे

#618

pacifier
पॅसिफायर्
चुचकारणी

#619

bell
बेल्
घंटा

#620

oil
ऑइल
तेल

#621

device
डिव्हाइस
उपकरण

#622

ladder
लॅडर्
शिडी

#623

helmet
हेल्मेट्
शिरस्त्राण

#624

pen
पेन्
पेन

lightbulb
लाईट्-बल्ब्
बल्ब

dictionary
डिक-श-नरी
शब्दकोश

magnet
मॅग्नेट
चुंबक

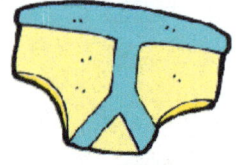

underpants
अंडर-पँट्स
अंडरपँट

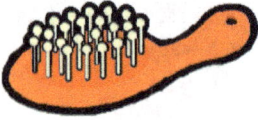

comb
कॉम्
कंगवा

bomb
बॉम्
बॉम्ब

microphone
मायक्रोफोन्
मायक्रोफोन

bedroom
बेडरूम्
झोपण्याचे खोली

sock
सॉक
मोज

microscope
मायक्रोस्कोप्
सूक्ष्मदर्शक

wood
वुड्
लाकूड

dartboard
डार्ट-बोड
डार्टबोड

plate
प्लेट
प्लेट

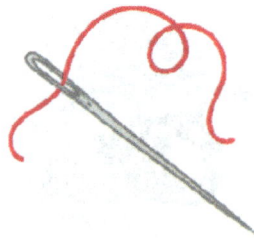

needle
नीडल
सुइ

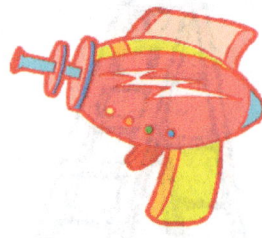

gun
गन्
बंदूक

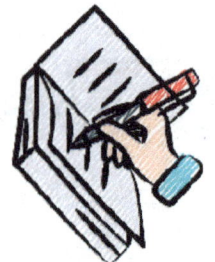

log
लॉग
लॉग

#641

strainer
स्ट्रे-नर
गाळण

#642

alcohol
अल्कोहोल
मद्य

#643

cactus
कॅक्टस्
कॅक्टस

#644

pajamas
पजामा
पायजमा

#645

mask
मास्क्
मुखवटा

#646

razor
रेजर
क्षौर

#647
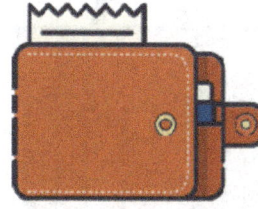
wallet
वॉलेट्
पाकीट

#648

engine
इंजिन्
इंजन

#649

rug
रग
गालीचा

#650

bookcase
बुक-केस
पुस्तक कपाट

#651
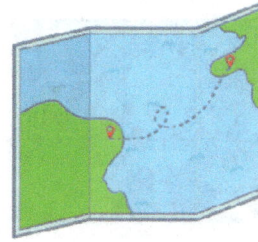
map
मॅप्
नकाशा

#652

cot
कॉट्
खाट

#653

glove
ग्लव्
हातमोजे

#654

window
विंडो
खिडकी

#655

machine
मशी-न
यंत्र

#656

doormat
डोर्मॅट
डोअरमॅट

#657

camera
कॅमेरा
कॅमेरा

#658

dress
ड्रेस्
ड्रेस

#659

telescope
टेलिस्कोप्
दूराबेण

#660

bracelet
ब्रेस-लेट्
कंगण

#661

knife
नाइफ्
चाकू

#662

briefcase
ब्रीफकेस्
ब्रीफकेस

#663

skirt
स्कर्ट्
परकर

#664

faucet
फॉ-सेट
नळ

#665

street
स्ट्रीट्
रस्ता

#666

bathroom
बाथ-रूम
स्वच्छतागृह

#667

barn
बान्
धान्याचे कोठार

#668

hall
हॉल
हॉल

#669

garden
गार्डन्
बाग

#670

brick
ब्रिक्
वीट

#671

palm
पाम्
पाम

#672
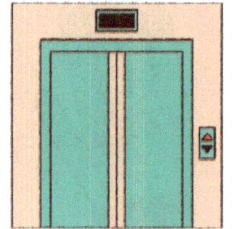
elevator
एलेवेटर
लिफ्ट

#673

sinks
सिंक्स
सिंक

#674

puddle
पडल्
डबकं

#675

wall
वॉल
भिंत

#676

garage
गॅरेज
गॅरेज

#677

bench
बंच
खंडपीठ

#678

fence
फेन्स्
कुंपण

#679

clothesline
क्लोथ्स-लाइन
कपड्यांची दोरी

#680

hose
होज
रबरी नळी

#681

attic
अॅटिक
पोटमाळा

#682

gravel
ग्रॅवेल
गवारे

#683

room
रूम
खोली

#684

treehouse
ट्री-हाउस
झाडाचे घर

#685
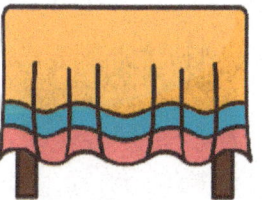
tablecloth
टेबल-क्लॉथ
टेबलक्लाथ

#686

mud
मड
चिखल

#687

rock
रॉक
दगड

#688

roof
रूफ
छप्पर

#689

leaf
लीफ्
पान

#690

bridge
ब्रिज्
पूल

#691

castle
कॅसल्
किल्ला

#692
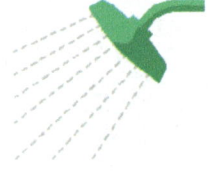
shower
शॉवर
शॉवर

#693

flower
फ्लॉवर्
फुल

#694

gate
गेट
गेट

#695

stone
स्टोन्
दगड

#696

sofa
सोफा
सोफा

#697

farm
फाम्
शेत

#698

windmill
विंड्-मिल्
पवनचक्की

#699

trash
ट्रॅश
कचरा

#700

hut
हट
झोपडा

#701

building
बिल्डिंग
इमारत

#702

escalator
एस्क-लेट-र
एस्केलेटर

#703

pool
पूल
तलाव

#704
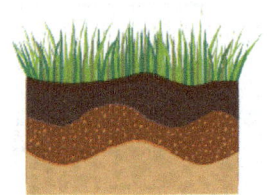
soil
सॉइल
माती

#705  **shelter** शेल-टर आश्रय	#706  **grass** ग्रास् गवत	#707  **pipe** पाइप नळ	#708  **road** रोड रस्ता
#709  **door** डोअर् दरवाजा	#710  **field** फिल्ड मैदान	#711  **ground** ग्राउंड् जमीन	#712  **house** हाऊस् घर
#713  **tombstone** टॉम्ब-स्टोन् समाधी	#714  **chimney** चिमनी धुराडं	#715 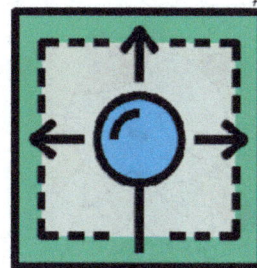 **area** ए-रिया क्षेत्र	#716  **curtain** कटन् पडदा
#717  **garbage** गाबेज कचरा	#718  **tree** ट्री झाड	#719  **nightstand** नाइट-स्टन्ड नाईटस्टॅंड	#720  **office** ऑफिस कायोलय

#721  home होम घर	#722  dust डस्ट् धूळ	#723  fountain फाउंटन कारंज	#724  hydrant हायड्रंट हायड्रंट
#725  tame टेम् वश करणे	#726  bathe बाथ आंघोळ करणे	#727  win विन् जिंकणे	#728  remember रिमेम्बर् आठवणे
#729  sick सिक्स् आजारी	#730  thank थंक् धन्यवाद	#731  avoid अवॉइड् टाळणे	#732  shake शेक हलवणे
#733  goodbye गुड्-बाय् निरोप	#734  sing सिंग गाणे	#735  drink ड्रिंक् पिणे	#736  hug हग् मिठी

#737

dart
डार्ट
डार्ट

#738

forbid
फॉरबिड्
मनाइ

#739

decrease
डिक्रेस्
कमी

#740

respect
रेस्पेक्ट
आदर

#741

beg
बेग्
भीक मांगणे

#742

fry
फ्राय
तळणे

#743

hide
हाइड्
लपवा

#744

talk
टॉक
गप्पा

#745

create
क्रिएट्
निर्माण करणे

#746

nap
नॅप्
डुलकी

#747

kiss
किस
चुंबन घेणे

#748

smile
स्माइल
हसू

#749

dream
ड्रीम
स्वप्न पाहणे

#750

follow
फॉल-लो
अनुसरण करणे

#751

buy
बाय
खरेदी करणे

#752

rob
रॉब्
दरोडा

#753

sew
सोव
शिवण

#754

crawl
क्रॉल
रांगणे

#755

achieve
आचेव्ह्
साध्य करणे

#756

solve
सॉल्व
उकलणे

#757

meet
मीट्
भेटो

#758

fly
फ्लाय्
उड्डाण

#759

read
रीड
वाचणे

#760

grill
ग्रिल
ग्रिल करणे

#761

open
ओपन्
उघडणे

#762

smell
स्मेल
वास घेणे

#763

cry
क्राय्
रडणे

#764

knit
निट
विणणे

#765

discover
डिस-का-वर
शोध

#766

walk
वॉक्
चालणे

#767

come
कम्
या

#768

enjoy
एन्जॉय
आनंद घ्या

#769
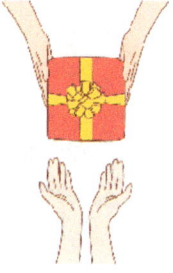
receive
रिसीव्
स्वीकारणे

#770

laugh
लाफ्
हसणे

#771

write
रायट
लिहा

#772

protect
प्रोटेक्ट्
संरक्षण

#773

give
गिव
देणे

#774

wait
वेट
वाट पाहा

#775

jump
जम्प्
उडी

#776

wash
वॉश्
धुणे

#777

grow
ग्रो
वाढ

#778

teach
टीच्
शिक्षण

#779

prevent
प्रो-वेंट
प्रतिबंध करा

#780

cook
कुक
स्वयंपाक

#781

believe
बिलेव्ह्
विश्वास ठेवणे

#782

improve
इम्प्रूव्
सुधारणा करणे

#783

run
रन्
धाव

#784

drill
ड्रिल
ड्रिल

#785

eat
इट्
खाणे

#786

bite
बाइट्
चावणे

#787

love
लव्ह्
प्रेम

#788

think
थिंक
विचार करणे

#789

stop
स्टॉप्
थांब

#790

climb
क्लाइम्ब
चढणे

#791

roast
रोस्ट
भाजणे

#792

develop
डव्हलप्
विकसित करणे

#793

clean
क्लीन्
स्वच्छ

#794

prefer
प्रे-फर
प्राधान्य

#795

prepare
प्रिपेअर्
तयार

#796

listen
लिसन
ऐकणे

#797

invest
इनवेस्ट
गुंतवणूक

#798

wag
वॅग्
हलवणे

#799

nibble
निब्बल्
तोडणे

#800

sit
सिट्
बस

dig
डिग्
खोदणं

build
बिल्ड्
बांधणं

play
प्ले
खेळ

snore
स्नोर
घोरणं

clap
क्लॅप्
टाळी वाजवणे

sleep
स्लीप
झोप

bake
बेक
बेक करणं

hurt
हट्
दुखणं

celebrate
सेलि-ब्रेट्
साजरा करणे

yawn
याॅन
जांभई

choose
चूझ्
निवडा

hello
हेलो
नमस्कार

speak
स्पीक्
बोला

sketch
स्केच्
रेखाचित्र

understand
अंडर-स्टॅन्ड्
समजणं

cut
कट
कापणं

#817

race
रेस्
शर्यत

#818

discuss
डिस-क्स
चर्चा करणे

#819

angry
ॲन्ग्री
राग

#820

help
हेल्प्
मदत

#821

close
क्लोज
बंद करणं

#822

watch
वॉच
घड्याळ

#823

boil
बॉयल
उकळणं

#824

music
म्युझिक्
संगीत

#825

piano
पियानो
पियानो

#826

trumpet
ट्रम्पेट
कर्णा

#827

horn
हॉर्न
हॉर्न

#828

violin
वायो-लिन्
व्हायोलिन

#829

xylophone
झायलोफोन
झायलोफोन

#830

jukebox
ज्यूकबॉक्स
ज्यूकबॉक्स

#831

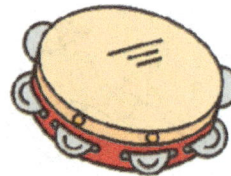

tambourine
तॅम-बो-रीन
डफ

#832

drum
ड्रम्
ढोल

#833

harp
हार्प
वीणा

#834

accordion
ॲकॉर्डियन
एकॉर्डियन

#835

saxophone
सॅक्सोफोन
सॅक्सोफोन

#836

guitar
गिटार्
गिटार

#837

drumstick
ड्रम-स्टिक
ड्रमास्टेक

#838

harmonica
हार्मोनिका
हार्मोनिका

#839

ukulele
उकूलेले
युकुलेल

#840

motorcycle
मोटर-सायकल
मोटारसायकल

#841

train
ट्रेन्
रेल्वे

#842

barrow
बॅरो
खबर

#843

balloon
बलून
फुगा

#844

bus
बस
बस

#845

kayak
काय-यॅक
कयाक

#846

submarine
सब-मा-रीन
पाणबुडी

#847

ship
शिप
जहाज

#848

boat
बोट
होडी

#849

firetruck
फायर-ट्रक
फायर ट्रक

#850

wagon
वॅगन
वॅगन

#851

helicopter
हेलि-कॉप-टर
हेलिकॉप्टर

#852

bicycle
बाय-सायकल्
सायकल

#853

plane
प्लेन्
विमान

#854

car
कार्
गाडी

#855

cart
काट
काट

#856

sled
स्लेड
स्लेज

#857

unicycle
युनि-सायकल
एक सायकल

#858

vehicle
व्होकल
वाहन

#859

scooter
स्कू-टर्
स्कूटर

#860

canoe
कॅनो
डांगा

#861

snowboard
स्नो-बोड
स्नोबोड

#862

sailboat
सेल्-बोट्
होडी

#863

airplane
एअर-प्लेन्
विमान

#864

bike
बाइक
दुचाकी

truck
ट्रक्
ट्रक

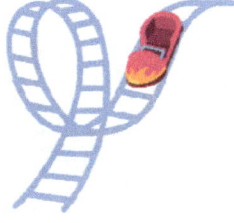

rollercoaster
रोलर-कोस्टर
रोलरकोस्टर

yacht
यांट
नौका

raft
राफ्ट
तराफा

skateboard
स्केटबोर्ड
स्केटबोर्ड

van
व्हॅन
व्हॅन

parachute
पॅरा-शूट्
पॅराशूट

subway
सब-वे
मेट्रो

ferry
फरी
फरी

rocket
रॉकेट्
रॉकेट

boxing
बॉक्सिंग्
बॉक्सिंग

acrobat
ॲक्रोबॅट
एक्रोबॅट

cycling
सायकालेंग
सायकालेंग

wrestling
रेसालेंग
कुस्ती

team
टाम्
संघ

fishing
फिशिंग्
मच्छीमारी

ball
बॉल
चेंडू

soccer
सॉकर्
फुटबॉल

fight
फायट
लढा

timer
टाइमर
टायमर

whistle
व्हिसल
शिट्टी

kite
काइट्
पतंग

racket
रॅ-िकेट
रॅकेट

dance
डान्स्
नाच

archery
आचरी
धनुर्विद्या

driving
ड्रायविंग्
गाडी चालवणे

racquet
रॅकेट
रॅकेट

climbing
क्लायमिंग्
चढणे

jogging
जॉगिंग्
धावणे

dumbbells
डम्ब्-बेल्स्
डंबेल

swimming
स्विमिंग्
पोहणे

golf
गोल्फ
गोल्फ

#897

dive
डाइव
डुबकी मारणे

#898

yoyo
यायो
यायो

#899

football
फुटबॉल
फुटबॉल

#900

ride
राइड
स्वार होणे

#901

hopping
हॉपिंग्
उड्या मारणे

#902

trampoline
ट्रॅम्पोलीन
ट्रॅम्पोलिन

#903

paddle
पॅडल
पॅडल

#904

surfing
सार्फिंग
सार्फिंग

#905

gymnastics
जिम्नॅस्टिक्स
जिम्नॅस्टिक्स

#906

wednesday
वेड-नेस-डे
बुधवार

#907

tuesday
ट्यूजडं
मंगळवार

#908

saturday
सॅटरडं
शानेवार

#909

sunday
संडं
रावेवार

#910

thursday
थसडं
गुरुवार

#911

monday
मंडं
सोमवार

#912

friday
फ्रायडं
शुक्रवार

#913

king
किंग्
राजा

#914

barber
बाबर्
न्हावी

#915

witch
विच्
चेटकीण

#916

pharmacist
फार-मा-सिस्ट
औषधनिर्माता

#917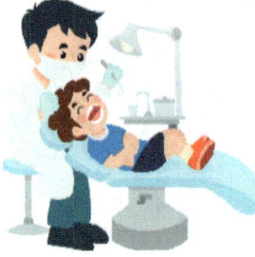

dentist
डाण्टेस्ट
दंतवैद्य

#918

entrepreneur
ऑन-ट्र-प्र-नूर
उद्योजक

#919

princess
प्रिन्सेस्
राजकुमारी

#920

leader
लीडर्
नेता

#921

doctor
डॉक्टर्
डॉक्टर

#922

knight
नाइट्
शूरवीर

#923

magician
मॉजीशयन्
जादूगार

#924

boss
बॉस्
मालक

#925

receptionist
रिसेप-श-निस्ट
रिसेप्शनिस्ट

#926

pirate
पायरेट्
समुद्री चाचां

#927

fisherman
फिशर-मॅन
मच्छीमार

#928

carpenter
कारपेन्टर्
सुतार

#929

nurse
नस्
पारिचारिका

#930

singer
सिंगर
गायक

#931

lawyer
लॉ-यर
वकील

#932

police
पो-लिस
पोलीस

#933

actor
ॲक्टर
अभिनेता

#934

photographer
फोटोग्राफर्
छायाचित्रकार

#935

army
आर्मी
सेना

#936

teacher
टीचर्
शिक्षक

#937

veterinarian
व्हेट-रि-ने-रि-अन
प्राणिवैद्य

#938

chef
शफ्
शेफ

#939

ghost
घोस्ट
भूत

#940

waiter
वटर्
वेटर

#941

politician
पॉलिटिशियन्
राजकारणी

#942

president
प्रेसिडेन्ट्
अध्यक्ष

#943

cop
कॉप्
पोलीस

#944

musician
म्युझिशियन्
संगीतकार

#945	#946	#947	#948
judge जज न्यायाधीश	optician ऑप-टिशे-न दृष्टीतज्ञ	florist फ्लॉ-रिस्ट फुलवाला	bartender बार-टेंडर बारटेंडर

#949	#950	#951	#952
accountant अॅकाऊंट-न्ट लेखापाल	butcher बुट्चर् कसाई	driver ड्राय-वर चालक	policeman पोलीसमॅन् पोलीस

#953	#954	#955	#956
plumber प्लंबर प्लंबर	bishop बिशप बिशप	hairdresser हेअर-ड्रेसर केशभूषा	writer राय-टर लेखक

#957	#958	#959	#960
miner माय-नर खानक	maid मेड घरकाम करणारी	cashier कॅश-यर कॅशियर	angel एन्जल् देवदूत

#961  artist आर्टिस्ट् कलाकार	#962  farmer फार्मर् शेतकरी	#963  secretary सेक-रि-टे-री सचिव	#964  baker बेकर् बेकर
#965  queen क्वीन् राणी	#966 color the word and the picture in pink white white व्हाइट पांढरा	#967 color the word and the picture in pink blue blue ब्लू निळा	#968  red रेड् लाल
#969 color the word and the picture in pink yellow yellow येलो पिवळा	#970 color the word and the picture in pink pink pink पिंक गुलाबी	#971 color the word and the picture in pink gray gray ग्रे राखाडी	#972 color the word and the picture in pink brown brown ब्राउन तपकिरी
#973 color the word and the picture in pink green green ग्रीन हिरवा	#974  cold कोल्ड थंड	#975  windy विं-डी वारा	#976  cloud क्लाउड ढग

#977

mountain
माउंटन्
डोंगर

#978

sunny
सनी
उन्हाळी

#979

galaxy
गॅलेक्सी
आकाशगंगा

#980

hot
हॉट्
गरम

#981

cloudy
क्लाउ-डी
ढगाळ

#982

rain
रेन्
पाऊस

#983

summer
समर्
उन्हाळा

#984
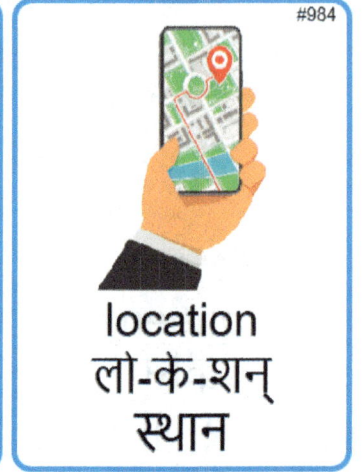
location
लो-के-शन्
स्थान

#985

globe
ग्लोब
ग्लोब

#986

volcano
वॉल्-कॅनो
ज्वालामुखी

#987

iceberg
आइसबग
हेमखंड

#988

moon
मून्
चंद्र

#989

world
वल्ड्
जग

#990

waterfall
वॉटरफॉल
धबधबा

#991

temperature
टेम्प्रा-चर
तापमान

#992

disaster
डिसॅस्टर
आपत्ती

#993

snowflake
स्नोफ्लेक्
हिमकण

#994

dawn
डॉन
पहाट

#995

snowy
स्नो-वी
हिमाच्छादित

#996

river
रिव्हर
नदी

#997

heat
हीट्
उष्णता

#998

coral
कोरल
कोरल

#999

moonlight
मूनलाइट
चंद्रप्रकाश

#1000

earth
अर्थ्
पृथ्वी

#1001

icicle
आइ-सिकल
हिमवर्षाव

#1002

star
स्टार्
तारा

#1003

climate
क्ला-इमेट
हवामान

#1004

forest
फॉरेस्ट
जंगल

#1005

stormy
स्टॉ-मी
वादळी

#1006

rainbow
रेनबो
इंद्रधनुष्य

#1007

loud
लाऊड्
मोठा आवाज

#1008

steam
स्टीम
वाफ

#1009

wave
वेव
लाट

#1010

nature
न-चर
निसर्ग

#1011

lake
लेक
तळे

#1012

wet
वेट्
ओला

#1013

quiet
क्वायेट्
शांत

#1014

thunder
थंडर्
मेघगर्जना

#1015

foggy
फॉ-गी
धुक

#1016

atmosphere
अॅट-मॉस्फिअर
वातावरण

#1017

ocean
ओशन
महासागर

#1018

snow
स्नो
बर्फ

#1019

quartz
क्वार्ट्झ
क्वार्ट्ज

#1020

smoke
स्मोक
धूर

#1021

coast
कोस्ट
किनारा

#1022

humid
ह्यू-मिड
आर्द्र

#1023

sun
सन्
सूर्य

#1024

sea
सी
समुद्र

#1025  rainy रे-नी पावसाळी	#1026  sound साउंड् आवाज	#1027  year इयर वर्ष	#1028  date डेट तारीख
#1029  midnight मिड-नाइट मध्यरात्र	#1030  week वीक आठवडा	#1031  noon नून मध्यान्ह	#1032  morning मॉर्नेंग् सकाळ
#1033  autumn ऑ-टम शरद ऋतू	#1034  month मंथ माहिना	#1035  night नाइट् रात्र	#1036  day डे दिवस
#1037  time टाइम वेळ	#1038  triangle ट्राय-एन्गल त्रिकोण	#1039  paint पेंट् रंग	#1040  passenger पॅसन्-जर् प्रवासी

#1041

lily
लिली
लिली

#1042

industry
इंडस-ट्री
उद्योग

#1043

dirt
डर्ट
माती

#1044

story
स्टोरी
कहाणी

#1045

government
गव्हर्नमेंट
सरकार

#1046

art
आर्ट
कला

#1047

haystack
हे-स्टॅक
गवताची गंजी

#1048

fern
फर्न
फर्न

#1049

winner
विनर
विजेता

#1050

funeral
फ्युनरल
अंत्यसंस्कार

#1051

anchor
अँकर
अँकर

#1052

product
प्रॉ-डक्ट
उत्पादन

#1053

circle
सर्कल्
वर्तुळ

#1054

ice
आइस
बर्फ

#1055

marble
माबेल
संगमरवरी

#1056

antler
अँटलर
शिंग

#1057

war
वार
युद्ध

#1058

octagon
ऑक्टा-गॉन
अष्टकोन

#1059

marigold
मॉरेगोल्ड
झेंडू

#1060

language
लॅन्वेज
भाषा

#1061

quiz
क्विज
प्रश्नमंजुषा

#1062

wheel
व्होल
चाक

#1063

message
मेसेज्
संदेश

#1064

honeycomb
हनी-कॉम्ब
मधाचा पोळा

#1065

jigsaw
जिग-सॉ
जिगसॉ

#1066

scale
स्केल
स्केल

#1067

christmas
ख्रिस्मस्
नाताळ

#1068

hive
हाइव
पोळ

#1069

crystal
क्रिस्टल
क्रिस्टल

#1070

cube
क्यूब
घन

#1071

game
गेम्
खेळ

#1072

movie
मुव्ही
चित्रपट

#1073

company
कंपनी
कंपनी

#1074

worker
वकर
कामगार

#1075

bubble
बबल
बुडबुड

#1076

feather
फदर
पंख

#1077

ivy
आयवा
आयव्ही

#1078

funnel
फनल
फनेल

#1079
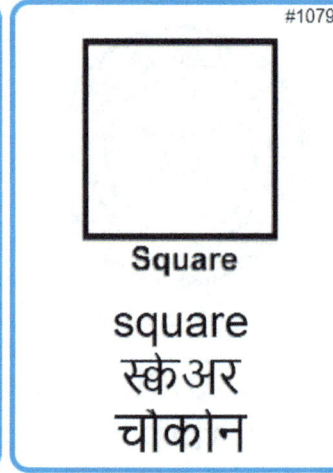
square
स्केअर
चौकोन

#1080

pair
पेर्
जोड

#1081

tulip
ट्युलेप
ट्यूलेप

#1082

nest
नेस्ट
घरटं

#1083

x-ray
एक्स-रे
क्ष-किरण

#1084

homework
होम-वक
गृहपाठ

#1085

boulder
बोल्डर
बोल्डर

#1086

painting
पेंट्-टिंग्
चित्रकला

#1087

package
पॅकेज्
पॅकेज

#1088

rose
रोज
गुलाब

#1089	#1090	#1091	#1092

point पॉइन्ट् बिंदू	fire फायर् आग	income इन-कम उत्पन्न	vine वाइन द्राक्षांचा वेल
#1093	#1094	#1095	#1096
		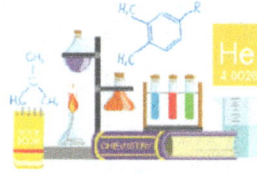	
song सॉंग् गाणं	number नम्बर् संख्या	chemistry केमिस्ट्री रसायनशास्त्र	sculpture स्कल्-प्चर् शिल्प
#1097	#1098	#1099	#1100

wedding वेडिंग् लग्न	customer कस्टमर ग्राहक	arrow अॅरो बाण	law लॉ कायदा
#1101	#1102	#1103	#1104

daisy डझी डझी	math मॅथ् गणित	birthday बथ-ड वाढादेवस	debt ड-ट कज

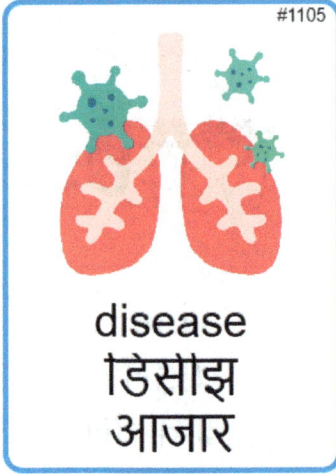

#1105

disease
डिसीझ्
आजार

#1106

error
एरर
चूक

#1107

news
न्यूज्
बातम्या

#1108

signature
सिग्नेचर्
स्वाक्षरी

#1109

user
यूझर्
वापरकर्ता

#1110

country
कंट्री
देश

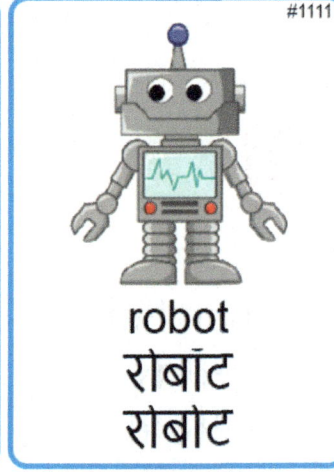

#1111

robot
रोबॉट
रोबोट

#1112

seashell
सी-शेल
साशेल

#1113

factory
फॅक्टरी
कारखाना

#1114

university
युनिव्हर्सिटी
विद्यापीठ

#1115

lab
लॅब
प्रयोगशाळा

#1116

library
लायब्ररी
ग्रंथालय

#1117

island
आयलॅन्ड्
बेट

#1118

cafe
कॅफे
कॅफे

#1119

supermarket
सुपर-मार्केंट
सुपरमार्केंट

#1120

shop
शॉप
दुकान

#1121

zoo
झू
प्राणीसंग्रहालय

#1122

hospital
हॉस्पिटल्
रुग्णालय

#1123

apartment
अपार्टमेंट
अपार्टमेंट

#1124

alley
अॅली
गल्ली

#1125

desert
डेजर्ट्
वाळवंट

#1126

school
स्कूल्
शाळा

#1127

market
माकेट
बाजार

#1128

estate
इस्टेट
मालमत्ता

#1129

highway
हाय-वे
महामाग

#1130

tunnel
टनल
बोगदा

#1131

classroom
क्लास-रूम
वग

#1132

city
सिटी
शहर

#1133

village
व्हिलेज
गाव

#1134

dam
डॅम्
धरण

#1135

hill
हिल्
टेकडी

#1136
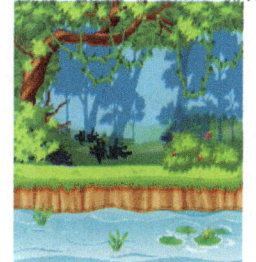
jungle
जंगल्
जंगल

#1137
lighthouse
लाइट-हाउस
दीपगृह

#1138
igloo
इग्लू
इग्लू

#1139
beach
बीच्
समुद्रकिनारा

#1140
airport
एअरपोर्ट
विमानतळ

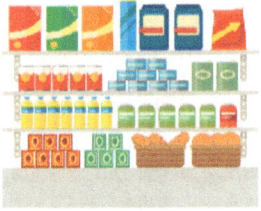

#1141
grocery
ग्रो-सेरी
किराणा दुकान

#1142
town
टाउन
शहर

#1143
watermill
वॉटर-मिल
पाणचक्की

#1144
pretty
प्रे-टी
सुंदर

#1145
sleepy
स्लीपी
झोपाळू

#1146
bad
बॅड्
वाइट

#1147
under
अंडर्
खालो

#1148
stack
स्टॅक
रचण

#1149
delicious
डिलीशस
चावष्ट

#1150
friendly
फ्रेन्ड्ली
मित्रत्वपूर्ण

#1151
shy
शाय्
लाजाळू

#1152
scary
स्करी
भयानक

#1153

unhappy
अन्-हॅप्पी
दु:खी

#1154

good
गुड्
चांगले

#1155

bored
बो-र्ड्
कंटाळलेला

#1156

sad
सॅड्
दु:खी

#1157

stinky
स्टिंकी
दुर्गंधी

#1158

proud
प्राउड्
अभिमान

#1159

impress
इम्प्रेस्
छाप पाडणे

#1160

big
बिग्
मोठा

#1161

stylish
स्टाइलिश्
फॅशनेबल

#1162

aggressive
अ-ग्रे-सिव
आक्रमक

#1163

smelling
स्मोलिंग्
वास

#1164

fat
फॅट्
जाड

#1165

joyful
जॉयफुल्
आनंदी

#1166

cute
क्यूट्
गोंडस

#1167

fresh
फ्रेश्
ताजं

#1168

happy
हॅप्पी
आनंदी

#1169  mad मॅड् राग	#1170  up अप् वर	#1171  strong स्ट्रॉन् मजबूत	#1172  history हिस्ट्री इतिहास
#1173  activity ऑक्टिव्हिटी क्रियाकलाप	#1174  friendship फ्रेंड-शिप मैत्री	#1175  freedom फ्रिडम स्वातंत्र्य	#1176 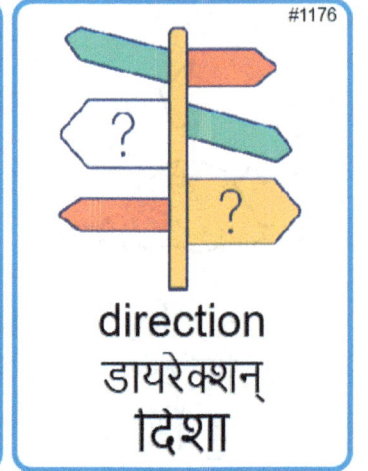 direction डायरेक्शन् दिशा
#1177  evil इव्हेल् वाईट	#1178  economics इकॉनॉमेक्स अर्थशास्त्र	#1179  health हेल्थ आरोग्य	#1180  wealth वेल्थ संपत्ती
#1181  society सोसायटी समाज	#1182  data डा-टा डेटा	#1183  safety सेफ-टी सुरक्षा	#1184  revenue रे-वन्यू उत्पन्न

#1185  profit प्रॉ-फिट नफा	#1186  goal गोल लक्ष्य	#1187  idea आय-डिया कल्पना	#1188  fact फॅक्ट् वस्तुस्थिती
#1189  question क्वेश्-चन् प्रश्न	#1190  security सेक्यूरिटी सुरक्षा	#1191  technology टेक-नॉल-जी तंत्रज्ञान	#1192  investment इनवेस्ट-मेंट गुंतवणूक
#1193  knowledge नॉ-लेज ज्ञान	#1194  ability अ-बी-लिटी क्षमता	#1195  education एज्युकेशन् शिक्षण	#1196  theory थी-अरी सिद्धांत
#1197  exam एग्जॅम् परीक्षा	#1198  energy एनर-जी ऊर्जा	#1199  entertainment एन्-टरटेन्मेंट् मनोरंजन	#1200  anxiety ॲन्झायटी चिंता

Made in the USA
Las Vegas, NV
12 March 2025